Words to Wealth: Mastering the Art and Business of Online Writing

Jeffrey T. Collins

TABLE OF CONTENT

1. Introduction
2. Evolution of Online Writing
3. Understanding the Online Writing Landscape
4. Developing Writing Skills
5. Building Your Online Presence
6. Monetizing Your Online Writing
7. Marketing and Promotion
8. Legal and Ethical Considerations
9. Scaling Up and Expanding Your Writing Business
10. Overcoming Challenges and Staying Motivated
11. The Future of Online Writing
12. Conclusions

INTRODUCTION

The Art and Business of Online Writing

Introduction: The Art and Business of Online Writing In today's digital age, the world of writing has experienced a profound transformation. The rise of the internet and the proliferation of online platforms have opened up new avenues for writers to showcase their creativity, connect with audiences, and pursue lucrative opportunities. Online writing has become a powerful medium that blends the realms of artistry and business, presenting a unique fusion of creative expression and entrepreneurial pursuits.

The purpose of this book is to explore the art and business of online writing, providing aspiring writers and professionals with insights, strategies, and practical advice to thrive in this dynamic landscape. By delving into various aspects of online writing, we aim to uncover the secrets to success, understand the evolving industry trends, and navigate the challenges that come with balancing artistry and commercial viability.

• **The Evolution of Online Writing:** The first chapter takes a step back to examine the evolution of online writing. We delve into the transition from traditional print mediums to the digital realm, exploring the factors that have influenced this shift and the implications it holds for writers. From the early days of blogging to the advent of social media platforms and content management systems, we explore how technology has shaped the online writing landscape, empowering writers to reach global audiences with ease.

•**Understanding the Online Writing Landscape:** To navigate the world of online writing effectively, it is crucial to gain a comprehensive understanding of the landscape. In this chapter, we explore the different forms of online writing, ranging from blog posts and articles to social media content and e-books. We delve into the vast array of platforms and channels available for writers to showcase their work, considering the advantages and challenges associated with each. Additionally, we explore the importance of identifying target audiences and niches, as well as staying abreast of current trends and best practices.

•**Developing Writing Skills for the Online World:** Writing for the online audience requires a distinct set of skills and techniques. In this chapter, we focus on developing essential writing skills that captivate online readers. We delve into the fundamentals of effective writing, such as crafting engaging and compelling content, employing storytelling techniques, enhancing clarity and coherence, and refining grammar and language usage. By honing these skills, writers can create compelling online content that resonates with their target audience and establishes their credibility.:

•**Building Your Online Presence:** Building a strong online presence is essential for any writer aspiring to succeed in the digital realm. In this chapter, we explore the process of establishing a writer's brand and crafting a compelling writer's bio that showcases expertise, personality, and unique voice. We delve into the strategies for optimizing online profiles, including author websites and social media platforms, to attract and engage readers. By building an online presence that aligns with their writing goals and target audience, writers can establish their authority and expand their reach.

•**Monetizing Your Online Writing:** While artistic expression is undoubtedly a driving force for writers, the potential to monetize their work is equally important. In this chapter, we delve into the various avenues for monetizing online writing. We discuss the business aspects of online writing, including understanding the value of content, exploring different revenue streams, and leveraging opportunities such as freelancing, ghostwriting, self-publishing, and affiliate marketing. By understanding the business side of online writing, writers can maximize their earning potential while staying true to their artistic vision.

•**Marketing and Promotion for Online Writers:** Writing a masterpiece is only the first step; effectively marketing and promoting one's work is equally vital. In this chapter, we explore the strategies and techniques for creating a robust marketing plan as an online writer. We delve into building an author website, harnessing the power of search engine optimization (SEO), utilizing social media platforms, and engaging with online writing communities and forums. Additionally, we discuss the importance of collaboration with other writers and influencers to expand one's reach and cultivate a dedicated audience.

• **Legal and Ethical Considerations:** As online writers, it is essential to navigate the legal and ethical considerations of the digital landscape. In this chapter, we examine topics such as copyright and intellectual property rights, understanding plagiarism and proper attribution, privacy and data protection, and adhering to ethical guidelines in online writing. We also address the challenges of handling negative feedback and managing trolls while maintaining professionalism and integrity.

• **Scaling Up and Expanding Your Writing Business:** For those seeking to take their online writing endeavors to the next level, scaling up and expanding the writing business becomes crucial. In this chapter, we explore strategies for managing workload, building a team of writers and editors, diversifying the writing portfolio, exploring international writing opportunities, and balancing artistic integrity with commercial success. By effectively scaling up the writing business, writers can achieve growth, sustainability, and increased professional opportunities.

•**Overcoming Challenges and Staying Motivated:** Writing, like any creative pursuit, comes with its share of challenges and hurdles. In this chapter, we address common obstacles faced by writers, such as writer's block, burnout, time management, handling rejections and criticism, finding inspiration, and cultivating a supportive writing community. By implementing practical techniques and maintaining a resilient mindset, writers can overcome challenges and sustain motivation on their writing journey.

•**The Future of Online Writing:** The final chapter of the book delves into the future of online writing. We explore emerging technologies and trends that will shape the industry and writers' experiences. From the impact of artificial intelligence and automation to the evolving reader preferences and advancements in publishing and distribution, we discuss how writers can adapt and embrace the opportunities that lie ahead.

Conclusion

In conclusion, the art and business of online writing offer writers a world of endless possibilities. This book serves as a guide, providing insights, strategies, and practical advice to navigate the dynamic landscape successfully. By balancing the artistic expression with the entrepreneurial mindset, writers can find fulfillment, reach wider audiences, and achieve both artistic and commercial success in the exciting world of online writing

CHAPTER 1

EVOLUTION OF THE ONLINE WRITING

Introduction: The evolution of online writing has revolutionized the way we consume and engage with written content. From the early days of the internet to the present digital age, the landscape of writing has undergone significant transformations, offering new opportunities and challenges for writers and readers alike. This chapter explores the journey of online writing, tracing its origins, key milestones, and the profound impact of technology on this evolving medium.

•The Birth of the Internet and the Emergence of Online Writing: The internet, as we know it today, emerged in the late 20th century, paving the way for a paradigm shift in how information is accessed and shared. With the birth of the World Wide Web in the 1990s, the online space became a breeding ground for written content. Early forms of online writing primarily consisted of static web pages and basic HTML coding. Websites served as platforms for individuals and organizations to share their thoughts, knowledge, and stories with a global audience.

•The Rise of Blogging and User-Generated Content: One significant milestone in the evolution of online writing was the rise of blogging in the early 2000s. Blogging platforms, such as Blogger and WordPress, empowered individuals to become publishers, enabling them to express their thoughts, share experiences, and offer insights on various topics. The ease of use and accessibility of blogging platforms fostered the emergence of a vibrant community of writers who found their voice in the digital realm.

•**Social Media and the Democratization of Online Writing:** The advent of social media platforms further democratized online writing, enabling anyone with an internet connection to publish and share their thoughts instantaneously. Platforms like Facebook, Twitter, and Instagram provided new avenues for writers to connect with readers on a global scale. Microblogging platforms, such as Twitter, encouraged concise and impactful writing, while visual-oriented platforms like Instagram allowed writers to combine their words with compelling visuals.

•**The Shift to Mobile and the Rise of Mobile Writing:** The proliferation of smartphones and tablets propelled the shift towards mobile writing. With the increasing dominance of mobile devices, writers had to adapt their content to suit smaller screens and cater to shorter attention spans. This gave rise to bite-sized content formats, such as listicles, microblogs, and interactive storytelling experiences that catered to on-the-go readers.

Mobile apps dedicated to writing, such as note-taking apps and writing prompts, also empowered writers to capture ideas and create content anytime, anywhere.

•Technology's Influence on Online Writing: Technological advancements have played a pivotal role in shaping the landscape of online writing. The development of content management systems, such as WordPress and Drupal, made it easier for writers to create and manage their websites without extensive technical knowledge. The rise of search engine optimization (SEO) techniques and tools helped writers optimize their content for higher visibility and reach. Additionally, advancements in artificial intelligence (AI) and natural language processing (NLP) have introduced automated writing tools, content generation algorithms, and language translation capabilities, further transforming the way writers approach their craft.

•**The Impact on Readers and Audience Engagement:** Online writing has empowered readers in unprecedented ways. With a vast array of online content available at their fingertips, readers have become active participants, engaging with writers through comments, sharing, and discussing content on social media. The democratization of online writing has also diversified the range of voices and perspectives, giving readers access to a broader spectrum of ideas and experiences.

•**The Future of Online Writing:** As we look to the future, the evolution of online writing shows no signs of slowing down. Emerging technologies, such as virtual reality (VR) and augmented reality (AR), have the potential to revolutionize the immersive storytelling experience. Artificial intelligence and machine learning will continue to enhance content creation, curation, and personalization. The rise of blockchain technology may also bring new possibilities for content ownership, copyright protection, and monetization.

Conclusion: The evolution of online writing has transformed the way we communicate, share knowledge, and connect with others. From the early days of static web pages to the dynamic world of social media and mobile writing, technology has been a driving force behind this evolution. Online writing has given rise to a diverse community of writers and readers, fostering creativity, collaboration, and engagement on a global scale. As technology continues to advance, the future of online writing holds immense potential for innovation, expanding the boundaries of storytelling, and shaping the way we consume and interact with written content.

CHAPTER 2

UNDERSTANDING THE ONLINE WRITING LANDSCAPE

Introduction: The online writing landscape is a vast and ever-evolving space that offers writers a plethora of opportunities to connect with audiences, share their ideas, and make an impact. This chapter aims to provide a comprehensive understanding of the online writing landscape, exploring the different forms of online writing, the platforms and channels available, the importance of identifying target audiences and niches, and the current trends and best practices that shape this dynamic ecosystem.

Different Forms of Online Writing: Online writing encompasses a diverse range of formats and genres that cater to various purposes and audiences. From informative articles and blog posts to creative fiction and poetry, writers have the freedom to choose the form that best suits their goals and writing style. Additionally, emerging formats like podcasts, video scripts, and interactive storytelling have opened up new avenues for writers to engage with audiences in innovative ways.

Platforms and Channels for Online Writing: The online writing landscape is characterized by a multitude of platforms and channels where writers can publish and showcase their work.

Blogging platforms like WordPress, Blogger, and Medium offer a straightforward way to start a personal blog and build an audience. Content management systems (CMS) such as Drupal and Joomla provide more robust options for creating websites with customized features. Social media platforms like Facebook, Twitter, and LinkedIn allow writers to share bite-sized content and connect with readers on a global scale. Furthermore, online publishing platforms and e-book marketplaces like Amazon Kindle Direct Publishing (KDP) and Smashwords offer avenues for self-publishing and distributing written works.

Identifying Target Audiences and Niches:
Understanding the importance of target audiences and niches is paramount in the online writing landscape. Identifying the specific group of readers who are most likely to resonate with a writer's content helps to tailor the writing style, tone, and topics to meet their needs and preferences. Niche writing, focusing on specific subjects or themes, allows writers to establish expertise, build a dedicated readership, and stand out in a crowded digital space.

Current Trends and Best Practices: Staying updated on the current trends and best practices is crucial for writers looking to thrive in the online writing landscape. Some prominent trends include the rise of long-form content, the importance of visual elements and multimedia integration, the growing demand for personalized and interactive experiences, and the need for mobile-friendly content. Best practices encompass elements like writing compelling headlines, utilizing search engine optimization (SEO) techniques, engaging with readers through comments and social media, and cultivating a consistent and authentic online presence.

Navigating SEO and Discoverability: Search engine optimization (SEO) plays a significant role in helping writers gain visibility and reach in the online writing landscape. Understanding keyword research, on-page optimization techniques, and the importance of backlinks can greatly enhance a writer's discoverability. Writers should also be mindful of user experience and ensure that their content is easily accessible, well-structured, and responsive across different devices.

Engaging with Online Writing Communities and Forums: Engagement within online writing communities and forums is essential for building networks, gaining insights, and fostering collaboration. Platforms like Goodreads, Wattpad, and Reddit provide spaces where writers can connect with fellow writers, share their work for feedback, participate in writing challenges, and learn from the experiences of others. Engaging with these communities can not only enhance a writer's skills but also provide opportunities for exposure and growth.

Ethical Considerations in Online Writing: Navigating the ethical considerations of online writing is crucial for maintaining professionalism and integrity. Proper attribution, respecting copyright and intellectual property rights, and upholding ethical guidelines when writing sponsored or promotional content are essential for building trust with readers and preserving the credibility of the writer.

Conclusion: Understanding the online writing landscape is fundamental for writers seeking success in the digital era. By exploring the different forms of online writing, platforms and channels available, identifying target audiences and niches, and staying abreast of current trends and best practices, writers can navigate this dynamic landscape with confidence. Engaging with online writing communities, embracing ethical considerations, and leveraging SEO techniques can further enhance a writer's visibility, reach, and impact in the online writing ecosystem. With a comprehensive understanding of the online writing landscape, writers can unlock the full potential of their creativity and effectively connect with readers worldwide.

CHAPTER 3

DEVELOPING WRITING SKILL FOR THE ONLINE WORLD

Introduction: In today's digital age, writing skills have become more important than ever, especially in the online world. With the proliferation of blogs, social media platforms, online publications, and e-commerce websites, the ability to effectively communicate through writing has become an essential skill. Whether you are a professional writer, a student, an entrepreneur, or an aspiring blogger, honing your writing skills for the online world can greatly enhance your success and impact. This article aims to provide a comprehensive guide to developing writing skills specifically tailored for the online environment. We will explore various aspects, including understanding the online audience, mastering the art of concise and engaging writing, leveraging technology and tools, and adopting effective editing techniques. By following these guidelines, you can become a proficient writer in the online world, creating content that captivates and resonates with readers across the globe.

Understanding the Online Audience: One of the fundamental aspects of developing writing skills for the online world is understanding the audience. Unlike traditional mediums, online readers have limited attention spans and are constantly bombarded with a vast array of content. Therefore, it is crucial to grab their attention quickly and hold it throughout your writing.To effectively engage the online audience, consider the following: Identify the target audience: Determine the demographics, interests, and preferences of your target audience. This understanding will help you tailor your writing style, tone, and content to resonate with them. **Use concise and scannable writing:** Online readers tend to skim through content rather than reading it word for word. Utilize short paragraphs, bullet points, subheadings, and bold keywords to make your writing scannable and easily digestible. Create compelling headlines: Craft catchy headlines that capture attention and promise value. A strong headline will entice readers to click and delve into your content.

Mastering Concise and Engaging Writing: In the online world, brevity and clarity are paramount. To master concise and engaging writing, consider the following tips:

Start with an outline: Before you begin writing, create an outline that organizes your thoughts and ensures a logical flow. An outline helps you stay focused and prevents your writing from becoming convoluted.

Be clear and straightforward: Avoid excessive jargon or complex sentence structures. Use simple and direct language that is easy for readers to understand. Remember, clarity should be prioritized over complexity.

Inject personality into your writing: Online readers appreciate authenticity. Develop your unique writing voice, and let your personality shine through your words. This will help you establish a connection with your readers and make your content more relatable.

. Embrace the Power of Editing and Proofreading: Editing and proofreading are essential steps in refining your writing for the online world. Once you have finished writing, take the time to review and revise your work. Look for grammatical errors, spelling mistakes, and awkward phrasing. Pay attention to the flow and coherence of your ideas, ensuring that each sentence contributes to the overall message. Consider using online grammar and spell-check tools, but remember that they are not foolproof and may miss certain errors. Where possible, ask a peer or professional to review your work for an objective assessment.

Engage in Continuous Learning and Improvement: Writing is a skill that can always be improved. Stay updated with the latest trends and developments in writing for the online world. Read articles, blogs, and books on the subject to gain insights and inspiration. Follow reputable writing communities and engage in discussions to exchange ideas and receive constructive feedback. Practice regularly by writing in different styles and genres to expand your repertoire. As you encounter challenges, embrace them as opportunities for growth and learning.

Conclusion: Developing writing skills for the online world is crucial in today's digital landscape. By understanding your audience, mastering clarity and conciseness, creating engaging content, utilizing SEO techniques,embracing editing and proofreading, and engaging in continuous learning, you can enhance your writing abilities and captivate your readers.Remember that writing is a process, and improvement takes time and practice. As you develop your skills, your confidence will grow, enabling you to communicate effectively in the online world and leave a lasting impact.

CHAPTER 4

DEVELOPING WRITING SKILLS

Enhancing Clarity and Coherence: Clarity and coherence are paramount in effective writing. This section explores techniques for organizing thoughts, structuring paragraphs, and creating logical flow within an essay or composition. It emphasizes the importance of topic sentences, transitional phrases, and concise expression to ensure clarity and coherence in writing.

IV. Mastering Different Writing Styles: Writing encompasses a variety of styles, each requiring specific skills and approaches. This section delves into different writing genres, including narrative, descriptive, expository, persuasive, and argumentative writing. It provides insights into the distinctive features of each style and offers practical exercises to develop proficiency in adapting to various writing contexts.

V. Developing Research and Critical Thinking Skills: Effective writing often necessitates research and critical thinking abilities. This section discusses strategies for conducting research, evaluating sources, and incorporating credible evidence into writing. It emphasizes the importance of developing analytical and critical thinking skills to present well-supported arguments and ideas.

VI. Improving Creativity and Expressiveness: Writing is not just about conveying information; it is also a medium for creative expression. This section explores techniques to enhance creativity in writing, such as brainstorming, freewriting, and using literary devices. It encourages individuals to experiment with different writing styles, prompts, and exercises to nurture their unique voice and writing style.

VII. Receiving and Implementing Feedback: Feedback is a valuable tool for growth and improvement in writing. This section highlights the significance of seeking feedback from peers, mentors, or writing communities. It offers guidance on providing constructive feedback and utilizing feedback effectively to revise and enhance written work.

VIII. Cultivating Regular Writing Practice: Consistent practice is crucial for developing and maintaining strong writing skills. This section provides tips for establishing a writing routine, setting achievable goals, and overcoming writer's block. It also suggests engaging in various writing exercises, prompts, and challenges to foster creativity and skill development.

IX. Embracing Editing and Proofreading: The final polish is achieved through careful editing and proofreading. This section emphasizes the importance of thorough editing to refine writing, eliminate errors, and improve clarity. It provides practical techniques and tools for effective self-editing and proofreading, as well as insights into seeking professional editing services when necessary.

Conclusion: Developing writing skills is a continuous process that requires time, effort, and dedication. By understanding the writing process, building a strong foundation, enhancing clarity and coherence, mastering different writing styles, developing research and critical thinking skills, nurturing creativity and expressiveness, seeking feedback, cultivating regular practice, and embracing editing and proofreading, individuals can significantly enhance their writing abilities. Whether for academic, professional, or personal purposes, effective writing skills empower individuals to articulate their thoughts with clarity, persuade and engage readers, and leave a lasting impact.

CHAPTER 5

BUILDING YOUR ONLINE PRESENCE

Content Creation and Curation: Compelling content material is the using pressure at the back of a a success on line presence. This section explores strategies for creating and curating high-quality content that captures the attention of your audience. It covers various content formats, such as blog posts, articles, videos, podcasts, and social media posts. It also delves into the importance of consistency, authenticity, and storytelling in content creation.

IV. Engage and Interact with Your Audience: Building a thriving online presence involves actively engaging and interacting with your audience. This section offers techniques for fostering meaningful connections with your followers, including responding to comments, initiating conversations, and participating in relevant online communities and forums. It emphasizes the value of listening to your audience, addressing their needs and concerns, and providing valuable insights and solutions.

V. Utilize Social Media Effectively: Social media platforms play a pivotal role in building an online presence. This section provides a comprehensive overview of leveraging social media effectively. It explores different platforms, their unique features, and the best practices for each. It covers strategies for growing your social media following, utilizing hashtags, optimizing content for different platforms, and monitoring analytics to refine your social media strategy.

VI. Establish Thought Leadership: Establishing yourself as a thought leader in your industry or niche is a powerful way to enhance your online presence. This section delves into the importance of thought leadership and offers strategies for positioning yourself as an authority figure. It explores techniques such as publishing guest articles, speaking at conferences, conducting webinars, and sharing valuable insights through your online platforms.

VII. Harness the Power of Search Engine Optimization (SEO): Search Engine Optimization (SEO) is instrumental in improving your online visibility. This section introduces the basics of SEO and provides practical tips for optimizing your online content. It covers keyword research, on-page optimization techniques, link building, and the importance of user experience in SEO.

VIII. Monitor and Manage Your Online Reputation: Maintaining a positive online reputation is essential for building a strong online presence. This section discusses strategies for monitoring and managing your online reputation. It explores tools and techniques for tracking mentions, responding to feedback and reviews, and addressing any negative content or controversies that may arise.

IX. Continuously Evolve and Adapt: Building an online presence is an ongoing process that requires continuous evolution and adaptation. This section emphasizes the importance of staying updated with the latest trends, technologies, and algorithms. It encourages you to regularly assess and refine your online presence strategy, experiment with new platforms and content formats, and embrace opportunities for growth and learning.

Conclusion: Building a compelling online presence is a valuable asset in today's digital landscape. By defining your online identity, establishing a strong online platform, creating and curating high-quality content, engaging with your audience, utilizing social media effectively, establishing thought leadership, harnessing the power of SEO, monitoring your online reputation, and continuously evolving and adapting, you can build an influential online presence that showcases your skills, expertise, and unique personality. Remember, building an online presence takes time and effort, but with consistency and a strategic approach, you can make a significant impact and open doors to new opportunities.

CHAPTER 6

MONETIZING YOUR ONLINE WRITING

Introduction: In the brand new virtual age, the net presents several possibilities for writers to monetize their skills and turn their passion for writing into a sustainable source of income. Whether you are a freelance writer, blogger, or aspiring author, understanding the strategies and avenues for monetizing your online writing is essential. This comprehensive guide aims to provide valuable insights and practical tips for effectively monetizing your online writing efforts.

I. **Establishing a Strong Online Presence:** Before diving into specific monetization strategies, it is crucial to establish a strong online presence. This section explores the importance of building a professional website or blog, optimizing your online profiles, and engaging with your audience. A strong online presence enhances your credibility and visibility, attracting potential clients and readers.

II. **Freelance Writing:** Freelance writing is a popular avenue for monetizing online writing skills. This section delves into the various aspects of freelance writing, including finding clients, negotiating rates, and delivering high-quality work. It explores different platforms and resources for discovering freelance writing opportunities, building a portfolio, and establishing long-term client relationships.

III. Blogging and Content Marketing: Blogging and content marketing provide opportunities to monetize your online writing through various channels. This section discusses strategies for monetizing a blog, such as sponsored posts, advertising, affiliate marketing, and selling digital products or services. It explores content marketing techniques, including creating valuable content, building an email list, and leveraging your expertise to attract clients or customers.

IV. Self-Publishing: Self-publishing offers writers the opportunity to monetize their work directly. This section explores the process of self-publishing e-books, print-on-demand books,and audiobooks. It covers topics such as writing, editing, formatting, cover design, distribution, and marketing. It also discusses platforms and resources for self-publishing success, as well as considerations for pricing and royalties.

V. Writing for Online Publications and Magazines: Writing for online publications and magazines allows writers to showcase their expertise and reach a broader audience. This section provides insights into pitching articles to online publications, understanding their guidelines, and writing compelling content. It explores the potential income streams, including upfront payments, royalties, and exposure opportunities through bylines and guest posts.

VI. Content Creation for Businesses and Brands

Many businesses and brands are in constant need of high-quality content to enhance their online presence. This section delves into the world of content creation for businesses and brands, including writing web copy, white papers, case studies, social media content, and email newsletters. It explores strategies for finding clients, setting rates, and delivering content that meets their specific needs and goals.

VII. Online Courses and Workshops: Online courses and workshops provide an avenue for monetizing your expertise and sharing your writing knowledge with others. This section discusses the process of creating and marketing online courses or workshops. It covers topics such as course development, platform selection, pricing, and marketing techniques to attract students and generate income.

VIII. Sponsored Content and Brand Partnerships: Sponsored content and brand partnerships offer writers opportunities to collaborate with brands and receive compensation for their work. This section explores the world of sponsored content, including sponsored blog posts, social media campaigns, and brand ambassadorships. It provides insights into finding relevant brand partnerships, negotiating agreements, and maintaining authenticity and transparency in sponsored collaborations.

IX. Diversifying Income Streams and Continual Growth: Diversifying income streams is essential for long-term success as an online writer. This section emphasizes the importance of exploring multiple monetization strategies and developing a portfolio of income-generating activities. It also encourages continual learning, staying updated with industry trends, and adapting to new opportunities to ensure ongoing growth and success.

Conclusion: Monetizing your online writing is an exciting and rewarding journey. By establishing a strong online presence, exploring avenues such as freelance writing, blogging, self-publishing, content creation for businesses, online courses, sponsored content, and brand partnerships, and diversifying your income streams, you can turn your passion for writing into a sustainable source of income. Remember, success in monetizing your online writing requires persistence, continuous learning, and the ability to adapt to the evolving digital landscape. With dedication and strategic efforts, you can achieve financial rewards while pursuing your writing dreams

CHAPTER 7

MARKETING AND PROMOTION

In today's competitive landscape, effective marketing and promotion are essential for individuals and businesses to stand out and reach their target audience. Whether you are an entrepreneur, artist, author, or running a small business, understanding the strategies and techniques for successful marketing and promotion is crucial. This comprehensive guide aims to provide valuable insights and practical tips for developing effective marketing campaigns, building brand awareness, and driving growth through strategic promotion.

I. **Understanding the Marketing Landscape**: Before diving into specific marketing and promotion strategies, it is important to understand the marketing landscape. This section explores the core concepts of marketing, including market research, target audience identification, and competitor analysis. It also introduces various marketing channels and platforms, such as traditional marketing, digital marketing, social media, and content marketing.

II. Developing a Marketing Strategy: A well-defined marketing strategy lays the foundation for successful marketing and promotion activities. This section delves into the process of developing a comprehensive marketing strategy. It covers elements such as setting goals and objectives, defining target audience personas, creating a unique value proposition, and establishing key performance indicators (KPIs). It also emphasizes the importance of aligning marketing strategies with overall business objectives.

III. **Branding and Positioning:** Branding and positioning play a vital role in marketing and promotion. This section explores the process of building a strong brand identity and positioning your product or service in the market. It covers topics such as brand messaging, visual identity, brand voice, and brand consistency. It also discusses techniques for differentiating your brand from competitors and creating a unique value proposition.

IV. Content Marketing: Content marketing is a powerful strategy for engaging with your target audience and building brand awareness. This section provides insights into creating valuable and relevant content that resonates with your audience. It covers techniques such as blog posts, articles, videos, podcasts, and infographics. It also explores content distribution strategies, SEO optimization, and measuring content marketing success.

V. Digital Marketing and Online Advertising: In the digital age, online advertising and digital marketing offer numerous opportunities for targeted marketing and promotion. This section explores various digital marketing channels, including search engine marketing (SEM), social media advertising, email marketing, and display advertising. It provides practical tips for optimizing online ads, leveraging analytics, and utilizing remarketing techniques.

VI. Social Media Marketing: Social media platforms have become indispensable tools for marketing and promotion. This section delves into effective social media marketing strategies. It covers topics such as creating engaging content, utilizing social media advertising, building a community, and measuring social media ROI. It also explores popular social media platforms and their unique features.

VII. Influencer Marketing: Influencer marketing has gained significant traction as a promotional strategy in recent years. This section discusses the concept of influencer marketing and provides insights into identifying relevant influencers, establishing partnerships, and measuring the effectiveness of influencer campaigns. It also explores the ethical considerations associated with influencer marketing.

VIII. **Public Relations and Media Outreach:** Public relations (PR) and media outreach are powerful tools for generating media coverage and enhancing brand visibility. This section explores the basics of PR, including crafting press releases, developing media lists, and building relationships with journalists and media outlets. It also covers techniques for organizing events, securing media coverage, and utilizing PR to manage crisis situations.

IX. **Measuring Marketing Success and Analytics:** Measuring the success of marketing efforts is crucial for optimizing campaigns and achieving desired outcomes. This section delves into marketing analytics and key metrics for tracking performance. It explores tools and techniques for monitoring website traffic, engagement metrics, conversion rates, and return on investment (ROI). It emphasizes the importance of data-driven decision-making and continuous optimization.

Conclusion Marketing and promotion are integral components of a successful business or personal brand. By understanding the marketing landscape, developing a comprehensive marketing strategy, leveraging branding and positioning, utilizing content marketing, digital marketing, social media marketing, influencer marketing, public relations, and measuring marketing success, individuals and businesses can effectively reach their target audience, build brand awareness, and drive growth. Remember, successful marketing and promotion require a combination of creativity, strategic thinking, and data-driven decision-making. With consistent effort, adaptation to market trends, and a deep understanding of your audience, you can achieve marketing success and take your business or personal brand to new heights.

CHAPTER 8

LEGAL AND ETHICAL CONSIDERATIONS

In today's complex and interconnected world, understanding and adhering to legal and ethical considerations is crucial for individuals and businesses alike. Whether you are an entrepreneur, professional, or content creator, operating within the boundaries of the law and upholding ethical standards is essential for maintaining integrity, building trust, and avoiding legal repercussions. This comprehensive guide aims to provide valuable insights and practical guidance on navigating legal and ethical considerations in various domains.

I. Understanding Legal Obligations:

Comprehending your legal obligations is the first step towards ensuring compliance and avoiding legal issues. This section explores different legal aspects, including contracts, intellectual property rights, data protection, consumer protection, and employment laws. It provides an overview of key legal concepts and considerations, highlighting the importance of seeking professional legal advice when necessary.

II. Protecting Intellectual Property:

Intellectual property (IP) rights are crucial for safeguarding original creations and innovations.

This section delves into the various types of IP, such as copyrights, trademarks, patents, and trade secrets. It explores strategies for protecting intellectual property, including registering copyrights and trademarks, drafting confidentiality agreements, and understanding licensing and fair use principles.

III. Ensuring Privacy and Data Protection: In an era of increased digital connectivity, privacy and data protection are critical considerations. This section discusses the importance of adhering to privacy laws, such as the General Data Protection Regulation (GDPR), and implementing robust data protection practices. It explores strategies for securing personal data, obtaining consent, and maintaining transparency in data collection and processing activities.

IV. Upholding Ethical Standards: Ethical considerations go beyond legal obligations and involve acting morally and responsibly. This section delves into ethical principles, such as honesty, integrity, transparency, and fairness. It explores ethical dilemmas that may arise in different domains, such as business, journalism, research, and content creation. It provides guidance on making ethical decisions and navigating potential conflicts of interest.

V. Maintaining Advertising and Marketing Compliances: Advertising and marketing activities are subject to specific regulations to protect consumers and ensure fair competition. This section explores advertising and marketing compliance considerations, including truth in advertising, endorsements and testimonials, social media disclosures, and avoiding deceptive practices. It emphasizes the importance of transparent and ethical marketing practices.

VI. Respecting Copyright and Fair Use: Copyright laws protect the rights of creators and content owners. This section discusses copyright principles, fair use exemptions, and the importance of respecting intellectual property rights. It explores strategies for avoiding copyright infringement, obtaining proper permissions, and utilizing copyrighted materials in a responsible and legally compliant manner.

VII. Engaging in Responsible Data Usage and Cybersecurity: As digital information becomes increasingly valuable, responsible data usage and cybersecurity are paramount. This section highlights the significance of protecting personal information, implementing cybersecurity measures, and adhering to data privacy laws. It explores best practices for data collection, storage, and disposal, as well as strategies for mitigating cybersecurity risks and responding to data breaches.

VIII. Ensuring Ethical Conduct in Research: Researchers and academics must adhere to ethical guidelines and principles when conducting studies and experiments. This section explores ethical considerations in research, such as informed consent, confidentiality, data integrity, and minimizing harm to participants. It also discusses the importance of obtaining ethical approval from relevant research ethics committees.

IX. Promoting Diversity, Equity, and Inclusion Creating an inclusive and equitable environment is an ethical imperative in today's society. This section explores strategies for promoting diversity, equity, and inclusion in various settings, such as the workplace, media, and content creation. It emphasizes the importance of fair treatment, equal opportunities, and combating discrimination and bias.

Conclusion: Legal and ethical considerations are foundational pillars for individuals and businesses operating in today's interconnected world. By understanding and adhering to legal obligations, protecting intellectual property, ensuring privacy and data protection, upholding ethical standards, maintaining advertising and marketing compliance, respecting copyright and fair use, engaging in responsible data usage and cybersecurity, ensuring ethical conduct in research, and promoting diversity, equity, and inclusion, individuals and organizations can build trust, maintain integrity, and navigate potential legal and ethical challenges. Remember, staying informed, seeking professional advice when needed, and consistently evaluating and adapting practices are crucial in upholding legal and ethical standards in an ever-evolving landscape.

CHAPTER 9

SCALING UP AND EXPANDING YOUR WRITING BUSINESS

a writer, scaling up and expanding your writing business is an exciting opportunity to increase your reach, impact, and profitability. Whether you are a freelance writer, a content creator, or an author, the potential for growth and expansion in the writing industry is vast. This comprehensive guide aims to provide valuable insights and practical strategies for scaling up and expanding your writing business effectively.

I. Assessing Your Current Position: Before embarking on the journey of scaling up and expanding your writing business, it is crucial to assess your current position. This section explores methods for evaluating your existing client base, income streams, strengths, and weaknesses. It emphasizes the importance of setting clear goals and developing a strategic plan that aligns with your vision for growth.

II. Diversifying Your Services and Offerings:
Diversifying your services and offerings is a key strategy for expanding your writing business. This section delves into different avenues for diversification, such as offering additional writing services, creating digital products or courses, providing consulting or coaching

services, or exploring new genres or industries. It provides insights into identifying market demand and capitalizing on emerging trends.

III. Building a Team and Outsourcing: Scaling up your writing business often requires expanding your team and leveraging the power of outsourcing. This section discusses the benefits of building a team and delegating tasks to qualified professionals. It covers topics such as hiring freelancers, virtual assistants, editors, and project managers. It also provides guidance on effective communication, collaboration, and workflow management.

IV. Developing Strategic Partnerships and Collaborations: Strategic partnerships and collaborations can accelerate the growth of your writing business. This section explores the potential for collaboration with other writers, publishers, agencies, or complementary service providers. It discusses the benefits of strategic partnerships, such as expanding your client base, sharing resources, and accessing new markets. It also provides tips for establishing and nurturing successful partnerships.

V. Expanding Your Online Presence: Expanding your online presence is crucial for scaling up your writing business. This section explores strategies for enhancing your visibility and reach through various online platforms, such as social media, blogging, guest posting, and podcasting. It discusses the importance of content marketing, search engine optimization (SEO), and building a strong personal brand to attract new clients and opportunities.

VI. Implementing Effective Marketing and Sales Strategies: Effective marketing and sales strategies are essential for scaling up and expanding your writing business. This section delves into various marketing techniques, such as creating a compelling website, utilizing social media advertising, email marketing, networking, and attending industry events. It emphasizes the significance of understanding your target audience, crafting persuasive messaging, and nurturing client relationships.

VII. Streamlining Operations and Workflows:

Streamlining operations and workflow is crucial for managing growth and maximizing efficiency. This section explores strategies for optimizing your writing processes, project management, and client communication. It discusses the importance of utilizing productivity tools, establishing clear workflows, and setting realistic deadlines. It also highlights the significance of continuous improvement and refining your operational systems.

VIII. Managing Finances and Pricing: Effective financial management is essential when scaling up your writing business. This section provides insights into managing your finances, budgeting, and setting pricing structures. It discusses strategies for determining fair rates, negotiating contracts, and tracking income and expenses. It also emphasizes the importance of maintaining profitability and financial sustainability during the expansion process.

IX. Continuous Learning and Professional Development: Continuous learning and professional development are crucial for the long-term success of your writing business. This section explores strategies for staying updated with industry trends, honing your writing skills, and expanding your knowledge. It discusses the importance of attending conferences, workshops, and webinars, joining professional associations, and seeking feedback from peers and mentors.

Conclusion: Scaling up and expanding your writing business offers immense opportunities for growth, impact, and financial success. By assessing your current position, diversifying your services, building a team, developing strategic partnerships, expanding your online presence, implementing effective marketing and sales strategies, streamlining operations, managing finances, and continuously learning, you can successfully navigate the challenges and embrace the opportunities of scaling up. Remember, scaling up is a dynamic process that requires careful planning, adaptability, and a commitment to delivering exceptional writing services. With the right strategies and a growth mindset, you can elevate your writing business to new heights and achieve long-term success.

CHAPTER 10

OVERCOMING CHALLENGES AND STAYING MOTIVATED

Life is full of challenges, both personal and professional, that can test our resolve and dampen our motivation. Whether you are pursuing a career, working on a personal goal, or navigating through daily life, it is essential to develop strategies to overcome obstacles and maintain motivation. This comprehensive guide aims to provide valuable insights and practical tips for overcoming challenges and staying motivated in the face of adversity.

I. Embracing a Growth Mindset: A growth mindset is the foundation for overcoming challenges and staying motivated. This section explores the concept of a growth mindset, emphasizing the belief that challenges and setbacks are opportunities for learning and growth. It provides strategies for cultivating a growth mindset, such as reframing failures, embracing feedback, and focusing on the process rather than the outcome.

II. Setting Clear and Meaningful Goals: Setting clear and meaningful goals is crucial for maintaining motivation and overcoming challenges. This section delves into the process of goal setting, emphasizing the importance of setting specific, measurable, attainable, relevant, and time-bound (SMART) goals. It provides strategies for aligning goals with personal values, breaking them down into manageable steps, and tracking progress.

III. Developing Resilience: Resilience is the ability to bounce back from setbacks and persevere in the face of challenges. This section explores strategies for developing resilience, such as cultivating a positive mindset, practicing self-care, building a support network, and reframing setbacks as learning experiences. It emphasizes the importance of self-reflection, adaptability, and seeking opportunities for growth in difficult situations.

IV. Managing Time Effectively: Time management is essential for staying motivated and overcoming challenges. This section provides insights into effective time management techniques, including prioritization, setting boundaries, creating a schedule, and eliminating distractions. It explores strategies for maximizing productivity, combating procrastination, and maintaining a healthy work-life balance.

V. Cultivating Self-Compassion and Mindfulness: Self-compassion and mindfulness play a vital role in overcoming challenges and maintaining motivation. This section delves into the importance of self-compassion, which involves treating oneself with kindness and understanding during difficult times. It explores mindfulness practices, such as meditation and deep breathing, to cultivate present-moment awareness and reduce stress. It also emphasizes the significance of self-care and nurturing one's well-being.

VI. Seeking Support and Building a Networks: Seeking support and building a network can provide invaluable resources and encouragement during challenging times. This section explores strategies for seeking support from friends, family, mentors, or support groups. It discusses the benefits of connecting with like-minded individuals, participating in communities or mastermind groups, and seeking guidance from experienced mentors or coaches.

VII. Embracing Failure and Learning from Setbacks: Failure and setbacks are inevitable in life, but how we respond to them determines our growth and resilience. This section discusses the importance of reframing failure as a learning opportunity and embracing a growth mindset. It explores strategies for extracting lessons from setbacks, maintaining a positive perspective, and using failures as stepping stones to future success.

VIII. Celebrating Milestones and Progress: Celebrating milestones and recognizing progress along the way is crucial for sustaining motivation and overcoming challenges. This section emphasizes the importance of acknowledging and celebrating even small victories. It provides strategies for setting milestones, rewarding oneself for accomplishments, and practicing gratitude to cultivate a positive mindset.

IX. Continuous Learning and Personal Development: Continuous learning and personal development are essential for staying motivated and overcoming challenges. This section explores strategies for pursuing knowledge and skills development, such as reading books, attending workshops or seminars, enrolling in courses, and seeking feedback from mentors. It emphasizes the importance of embracing a growth mindset and being open to new experiences.

Conclusions: Overcoming challenges and staying motivated are lifelong journeys that require perseverance, self-reflection, and the adoption of effective strategies. By embracing a growth mindset, setting clear and meaningful goals, developing resilience, managing time effectively, cultivating self-compassion and mindfulness, seeking support, embracing failure, celebrating milestones, and pursuing continuous learning, you can navigate challenges and maintain motivation in all areas of life. Remember, challenges are opportunities for growth, and staying motivated is a choice. With determination and a proactive mindset, you can overcome obstacles and achieve your goals, finding fulfillment and success along the way.

CHAPTER 11

THE FUTURE OF ONLINE WRITING

The digital age has revolutionized the way we consume and interact with content, shaping the future of online writing. With technological advancements and evolving consumer behaviors, the landscape of online writing is constantly changing. This comprehensive guide aims to provide insights into the future of online writing by exploring emerging trends, innovations, and opportunities for writers in the digital realm.

I. Rise of Artificial Intelligence in Writing: Artificial Intelligence (AI) is poised to have a significant impact on the future of online writing. This section explores the integration of AI in writing processes, such as AI-powered content generation, automated editing tools, and intelligent language processing. It discusses the potential benefits and challenges of AI in writing, as well as its implications for content quality, creativity, and the role of human writers.

II. Evolving Content Formats and Mediums: The future of online writing will witness the emergence of new content formats and mediums. This section explores trends such as interactive content, immersive storytelling, augmented reality (AR), and virtual reality (VR) experiences. It discusses the potential for engaging and immersive narratives that leverage technology to captivate and connect with audiences in novel ways.

III.   Personalization   and   Audience Engagement: As online writing evolves, personalization and audience engagement will become increasingly important. This section explores the trend of tailoring content to individual preferences and interests, leveraging data analytics and user insights. It discusses strategies for creating personalized experiences, such as adaptive content, customized recommendations, and interactive storytelling that allows readers to shape the narrative.

IV. Collaborative and Interactive Writing Platforms: The future of online writing will see the rise of collaborative and interactive writing platforms. This section explores the potential for co-creation, crowd-sourcing, and collective storytelling platforms that allow writers and readers to collaborate in real-time. It discusses the advantages of collaborative writing, such as diverse perspectives, collective intelligence, and community building.

V. Emphasis on Authenticity and Transparency: In an era of misinformation and fake news, authenticity and transparency will be crucial in the future of online writing. This section explores the trend of building trust through authentic storytelling, transparent sourcing, and ethical practices. It discusses strategies for combating misinformation, ensuring accuracy, and promoting ethical content creation and distribution.

VI. Monetization and New Revenue Streams: The future of online writing will present new opportunities for monetization and revenue streams. This section explores emerging models such as micro-payments, subscription-based content, membership platforms, and blockchain-based solutions for fair compensation and copyright protection. It discusses the potential for writers to diversify their income sources and establish sustainable careers in the digital landscape.

VII. Global Reach and Cross-Cultural Exchange: The internet has made it possible for writers to reach global audiences, transcending geographical boundaries. This section explores the trend of cross-cultural exchange, where writers can connect with readers from different parts of the world and explore diverse perspectives. It discusses the potential for cultural exchange, translation services, and platforms that bridge language barriers, fostering a more connected and inclusive global writing community.

VIII. Ethical Considerations and Digital Responsibility: As online writing continues to evolve, ethical considerations and digital responsibility become paramount. This section explores the need for ethical content creation, including responsible AI usage, protection of user data and privacy, combating online harassment, and promoting inclusive and diverse representation in online writing. It discusses the importance of digital literacy and responsible practices to maintain the integrity of online writing.

IX. Continuous Adaptation and Lifelong Learning: The future of online writing will require writers to embrace continuous adaptation and lifelong learning. This section emphasizes the importance of staying updated with technological advancements, industry trends, and evolving reader preferences. It discusses the need for writers to cultivate a growth mindset, embrace new tools and platforms, and pursue professional development to thrive in the dynamic digital landscape.

Conclusion: The future of online writing holds immense potential and opportunities for writers. With the rise of AI, evolving content formats, personalization, collaborative platforms, authenticity, new monetization models, global reach, and ethical considerations, writers can navigate the changing landscape and connect with audiences in innovative ways. Adapting to technological advancements, embracing ethical practices, and continuing to learn and grow will be crucial for writers to succeed in the future of online writing. By leveraging emerging trends and harnessing the power of digital tools and platforms, writers can forge new paths, create impactful content, and shape the future of the online writing industry.

www.ingramcontent.com/pod-product-compliance
Lightning Source LLC
Chambersburg PA
CBHW072131270726
48661CB00019BA/1603